Accepting

CHOSEN

Marnisha Hunt

ISBN 979-8-89345-666-0 (paperback)
ISBN 979-8-89345-667-7 (digital)

Christian Faith Publishing
832 Park Avenue
Meadville, PA 16335
www.christianfaithpublishing.com

Printed in the United States of America

Hi, Stinka Butt! Mommy's very first book, aren't you proud? You taught me self-love and self-worth. Everything I do is for you. You are my world. To my aunt Betty and uncle Collis, thank you for all you did for us. You left a lifelong impact on who we are. I will always love you guys. And to Mr. and Mrs. Watters, I would not be the woman I am today if it wasn't for the example you set in my life. I love you so much.

DE-CON-STRUC-TION:

Taking to pieces; breaking down or analyzing something to discover its true significance.

Prologue

I remember being between the ages of five and seven, I loved going to church every Sunday. I don't know why I loved it so much, but I had to be there. Something about it felt so comforting. It felt like home, like it was where I belonged. One Sunday, I remember it so clearly, they passed around communion, and I remember the pastor saying that the cracker symbolized Jesus's body and the grape juice symbolized His blood. Young and innocent minded, I looked at the cracker and the juice and thought, *Ew, I'm about to eat this man named Jesus!* But for some reason, I wanted to be a part of this seemingly secret society. No one in my family had ever talked about this, so I wanted to know just how real it was. The pastor continued saying, "Once you eat His body and drink His blood, He will always be inside of you." So I drank and ate, and I remember finishing the cracker and juice, wondering if that statement was true and what my life would look like from that point on.

I officially accepted the Lord into my heart at the age of twelve years old. I was in my third foster home at the time, and I didn't understand why my life was turning out the way that it was. Away from my mom, away from my family, I was being torn apart so young, and I didn't understand why. I couldn't fathom the Lord's ways, but I longed for comfort. So I got saved.

The Holy Spirit was like fire in me. I couldn't contain it, couldn't control it. My mind, my heart, everything became…more pure. I always say around this time of my life, I knew that Jesus raised me. It was so beautiful and so real. I loved church, and I loved Jesus. Friends in school would call me Pastor Marnisha because I carried the Bible to school in my purse! Talk about being on fire for the Lord.

Being saved and growing in God had become all that I knew. The pain of being ripped away from my mom subsided, but it remained in the deepest parts of me. I'm not sure if it was because of the pain in my life or if it was true curiosity, but a part of me knew I wanted a taste of that other life. The one they sang about in the songs. I wanted to know what sex felt like. I wanted to know how fun partying was. I wanted to know if these things were as satisfying as they made them seem. Only twelve years old and I knew that at some point I would put Jesus down and pick the world up.

Who knew it would happen so soon. Almost two years later, my brothers and I were taken from the foster home we were in. I had become so comfortable and attached to my now godparents that when they got snatched away from me, it hurt. My world was changing all over again. I was so confused. I thought we had found a permanent home. I thought God wouldn't do this to me again. I cried out to Him, I prayed, I worshiped. I had to be strong for myself and my brothers. I wanted them to believe that God would get us out of this unfamiliar, uncomfortable place. I spent ten months in my fourth foster home waiting for God to do something, anything. I grew angry and eventually numb.

By the age of fifteen, I was moving states to start a new life. This new life had me spiritually torn in two. I wanted to keep living saved, but everything was so new and exciting. I had never experienced life like this before. I was so well taken care of, so spoiled. I was living with actual family of mine, and it was a beautiful feeling. I was free— at least from the foster system. Spiritually, I wasn't free. I was at the beginning stages of my own bondage. Outside, I was bright, bubbly, and happy, but inside, I was fighting for my life.

I never really knew sin up until that point. I would sin constantly and feel terrible about it. After every sin, I would ask for forgiveness, but Satan would taunt me, condemn me, and lie to me. I stopped reading my Word, and because I couldn't fight his lies with the truth, I listened. I believed him when he said God was angry with me. I believed him when he said I couldn't do anything right.

I believed him when he said God didn't want anything to do with me if I wasn't living right. So I began training myself not to talk to God at all. If I knew I had sinned or that I was going to sin, I would completely ignore Him. I didn't feel worthy enough to even whisper a word His way. I just kept falling deeper into this hole of a lifestyle. As I sank lower and lower into deception, my will to fight was disappearing. I was losing the fight. I couldn't talk to the only person that could save me from sinking, because the enemy had me believing that talking to God was pointless. With no Savior and no fight left, I became my own god.

RE-CON-STRUC-TION:

a thing that has been rebuilt after being damaged or destroyed; the act or process of rebuilding, repairing, or restoring something.

Perfect Love

I took you from the ends of the earth, from its farthest corners
I called you. I said "you are My servant." I have chosen you
and have not rejected you. So do not fear, for I am with you;
do not be dismayed for I am your God. I will strengthen you
and help you; I will uphold you with My righteous right hand.

—Isaiah 41:9–10

Restoration…redemption…refuge. It all happened one night while I was studying. God had spoken directly to me through that scripture, and for the first time in my life, I heard Him so clearly. My soul was lifted. Everything was so clear. My heart burst open, and I could finally accept His unfailing, unconditional, unwavering love for little ole me. I wept, because from fifteen to twenty-five, I believed Satan's lies. Ten years, I believed God didn't want anything to do with me if I wasn't holy. For ten years, I couldn't fathom Jesus loving me *no matter what.* I didn't believe His love was a gift and that I didn't have to work for it. I couldn't accept that I was chosen. Truthfully, I didn't want to accept it. I was resentful toward God because of how my life had been growing up. Looking back, I see that I ran from Him for so long because I was angry with Him and I didn't trust Him with my life; I didn't know Him.

It had not been enough to know that Jesus died for me. It had not been enough to have the Holy Spirit within me like fire. It had not even been enough to grow up in church. I needed Jesus on a personal level. I needed Him to stop my world and open my heart to

His true nature and what walking with Him really meant. And He did just that.

From a very young age, I knew I was different from everyone around me. In a way, I knew I was called, but it takes perfect love to accept that call. The Bible says perfect love drives out fear, and fear was what my walk in Christ was rooted in. Fear of not being holy enough, fear of going to hell, and most of all, fear of not living up to who He's called me to be. In Isaiah 41:10, God says, "Do not fear, for I am with you." I left Him, but He never left me. I had no reason to fear. He was there the whole time. Second Timothy 1:7 also says,

> For God has not given us a spirit of fear, but
> of power, and of love and of a sound mind.

It's one thing to have the "fear of the Lord" inside of you. That's just reverencing the Master Himself. But to have fear as the foundation of your relationship with Him contradicts salvation completely. John 8:36 says, "Whom the Son sets free is free indeed." There is *freedom* in Jesus, not fear. Restitution came to me that night and love had become my foundation; it changed everything. I walked more boldly. There was a confidence about me that I never had before, and it was because I had been established in *perfect love*. Since we know that God has not given us a spirit of fear, what does He mean when He says He gave us power, love, and a sound mind?

Power: Through Jesus, God has given us the capacity and the ability to live this life! To see and to believe! To speak things into existence. He's given us power and authority through the Holy Spirit to accept the calling on our lives (Luke 10:19).

Love: "Love is…patient, love is kind, it does not envy, it does not boast, it is not proud. It does not dishonor others, it is not self-seeking, it is not easily angered, it keeps no record of wrongs. Love does not delight in evil, but rejoices with the truth. It always protects, always trusts, always hopes, and always perseveres. Love never fails" (1 Corinthians 13:1–8).

That is God's character completely, and that is who we ourselves are called to be.

Sound Mind: A peaceful mind. One that leans on and trusts every word God has spoken. A sound mind takes every thought captive and brings it under the authority of Jesus. A sound mind trusts wholeheartedly in the Lord.

Accepting chosen means rejecting the lies of the enemy. God's words hit me like a ton of bricks that day when He reminded me that He chose me and that He did not reject me. That He was my God and not myself or any of my circumstances. Despite every sin up until that point and despite how I thought He wanted to give up on me after so many times of asking forgiveness and repeating the same sin. Even after becoming my own god and ignoring Him for years, He still loved me so much, He brought me back to Him.

For I am convinced that neither death nor life,
neither angels nor demons, neither the present nor the future,
nor any powers, neither height nor depth, nor anything
else in all creation, will be able to separate us from
the love of God that is in Christ Jesus our Lord.

—Romans 8:38–39

The Good News!

God sent Jesus to earth to die for us so that we could go *freely* to the throne despite ourselves, despite our sin. Jesus dying and becoming that perfect love now intercedes for us and transforms us through His power alone, so that we are blameless in the sight of our all-powerful, almighty, all-knowing God. So then there is no condemnation for us who love Jesus. Jesus covers it all in perfect love! It's okay to accept God's gift of love and His perfect will despite where we are on our journey. Our only job is to keep our eyes on the Lord Jesus and to continue holding His hand so that we are continuously being transformed and renewed by perfect love. Grasping hold of this truth with all of your heart, mind, and soul is how you begin to accept being chosen.

Face Your Fear

Where have you struggled in your walk with God? Dig deep and be completely honest. Whether it is through rebellion, disobedience, or struggling with fear, there is always a root to the problem. Before writing, ask God to show you yourself like never before. Have faith that He will do it!

Exercise: Begin keeping a prayer journal, pouring out your deepest feelings about any and every subject. It is so freeing. Write in it every day. Eventually, you will be eager to write and get all of your feelings out on paper. This is how your prayer life should come to look and feel.

CHOSEN:

having been selected as the best or most appropriate.

Before I formed you in the womb, I chose you,
before you were born I set you apart.

—Jeremiah 1:5

God's Elect

It took years for me to realize and accept that I couldn't be like everyone else. I couldn't do what they did, and I most definitely couldn't get away with the things everyone else could. I remember at fifteen, I tried sneaking out of the house. The only reason I did it was because my brother would do it all the time and he never got caught. So one night, I got brave and decided to sneak out of my room window to go meet with some boy. By the time I got back, my aunt was waiting for me at the front door with my window screen in her hand. This was only one out of many times God tried to show me that I was set apart.

When you're chosen, God will constantly show you. He won't stop tugging on your heart. If you are truly one of His own, He will chase you down until you stop running. From experience alone, I can say nothing worked out the way that I wanted it to while in my running season. Life just didn't flow when I tried to do things my way. I was always met with opposition. Apart from the Lord, I had no fruit from the lifestyle I was living. I was nothing without Him, and it showed. Jesus says in John 15:5, "I am the vine; you are the branches. If you remain in me and I in you, you will bear much fruit; apart from me you can do nothing."

Every time you run from God, He will show you exactly why it's a bad idea. We were not created to live apart from Him. Like a fish on dry land, we were not meant to live outside of the *Living Water.* Look at depression, anxiety, and suicide rates. Life apart from Him is darkness. It's empty, void of meaning and purpose. That alone has been proven time and time again in my own life.

Since you are chosen, set apart for His will and purpose, any identity outside of Him is no identity at all. When God gave me this revelation, it forced me to go back to the beginning…when I decided to pick the world up and put Jesus down. I picked up smoking habits and drinking habits. I had sex, I partied, even got pregnant out of wedlock and had my daughter. All of these things I thought made up who I was. From the experiences I had, losses I took, heartbreaks and struggles, I thought, *This is just my life, this is who I am.* But I knew better. I knew most of those things wouldn't have happened if I had not been running away from God. running away from my calling. I ran away in rebellion because I was angry with Him. I didn't want His identity for my life, I wanted to create my own. And boy. did that cost me.

So if you're not who you think you are…who are you? All throughout the Bible, God continues to define who you are *in* Him.

- Deuteronomy 14:2 says, "For you are a people holy to the Lord your God. Out of all the people on the face of the earth, the Lord has chosen you to be His treasured possession."
- Leviticus 20:26 says, "You are to be holy to me because I, the Lord, am holy and have set you apart from the nations to be my own."
- Second Corinthians 5:17 says, "Therefore if anyone is in Christ, He is a new creation. The old has passed away; behold, the new has come.

God continually tells us who He predestined us to be in Him. His desire for us is to take on this identity. "Before I formed you in the womb I knew you. Before you were born I set you apart." God is saying before you even became a tiny fetus in your mother's womb, He knew you. The real you. We are spirits inhabiting fleshy bodies. That means He knew your spirit! *That* is who you truly are.

Being chosen means to be set apart from this world. A lot of Christians, at some point, feel like walking with Jesus is boring. As a young Christian, I definitely did. The world seems as if it has so much more fun and satisfying things in it. So it lures us in. That is *deceit*. Whether we are aware of it or not, our souls yearn for the living God. That is why the world chases fame and riches. They think it will eventually satisfy the deep yearning within. They experience an ongoing identity crisis. To them, money equals happiness or fulfillment. Ultimately, they're trying to fill the void only God can fill. Partying, sex, drugs—they're all temporary counterfeit gods.

Have you ever wondered why after sex or the morning after the club you feel yucky? You feel depressed and anxious or like you need more. This is one of the enemy's tactics. He knows that sin is addictive. After one hit, you need more and more. That is how he entraps you. Constantly chasing a high from the immediate satisfaction of sin. After doing this for so long, you eventually start going down a dark hole because your *spirit* longs for more. It thirsts for *Living Water*, and nothing of this world can quench that thirst. The pattern of the world is to chase after money and fame. To find happiness indulging in things the flesh desires. To serve oneself. But that is not who *you* are. That is not who God called you to be.

In the words of the lovely Bishop Marc L. House, "Jesus came into the culture and disrupted it. He didn't come into the world and become a part of it." So when the Bible says God called us to be set apart, He means literally. Come out of the crowd and *die* to yourself. It is the exact opposite of the culture. Your identity in Christ is the real you. Starving your flesh of the things of this world. Looking to Jesus to cleanse you of all of your past or present sin. This may seem like an impossible task for *you*, but with God, *nothing* is impossible. This is the foundation of salvation. The reason God sent His only son Jesus. For us to *die* to our flesh and *live* through Him.

We find our true selves and purpose through Jesus. It's not an easy walk by any means, and you will constantly battle with your flesh. We are only human. Our nature is sin. We will never be perfect, and that's okay. So when you stumble, don't stay on the ground. Get up and keep going. Remember that God is with you *and* within you. He is an ever-present help in times of trouble. You can walk this walk by never letting go of His hand. Don't fear your calling, don't fear your shortcomings, and don't fear His will. Embrace it all. Your life *in* Him is so beautiful.

> In His great mercy He has given us new birth into a living hope through the resurrection of Jesus Christ from the dead, and into an inheritance that can never perish, spoil or fade. This inheritance is kept in heaven for you, who through faith are shielded by God's power until the coming of the salvation that is ready to be revealed in the last time. In all this you greatly rejoice, though now for a little while you may have had to suffer grief in all kinds of trials. These have come so that the proven genuineness of your faith—of greater worth than gold, which parishes even though refined with fire—may result in praise, glory and honor when Jesus Christ is revealed. Though you have not seen Him, you love Him; and even though you do not see Him now, you believe in Him and are filled with an inexpressible and glorious joy, for you are receiving the end result of your faith, the salvation of your souls.

—1 Peter 1:3–9

Carry Your Cross

How do you feel about the things of this world versus your relationship with God? Has it been hard for you to let these things go? If so, why do you think that is?

Do you feel like you're chosen? Why or why not? After writing, pray and ask God to establish your identity *in* Him. To be *rooted* in Him. Ask Him questions; vent to Him about where you are on your journey. With a sincere heart, talk but also *listen*. Sit in silence, and allow Him to fill you.

Exercise: Begin trying to fast more often. At least once a week. Give up something—social media, food, soda, etc.—for that entire fast. As you fast, begin to ask God for His power to remove things in your life that don't glorify or honor Him (ex: smoking, drinking, sexual impurity). A fast is one way to build intimacy with God. Allow His desires to become your desires. Remember that this walk is a lifelong journey.

Notes

A Journey of Love

Since I was twelve years old, one thing has proven itself to be true over and over again. Just because you're chosen doesn't mean you won't struggle with sin. If you allow him to, the enemy will creep into your thoughts and influence your emotions. If we are not sober-minded and aware of ourselves and aware of his tactics, we will fall. All of my life, there's been a war inside of me: my spirit crying out to God and my flesh crying out to sin. Trauma and pain will intensify both.

I believe there is trauma in us all. Things that happened to us that made us the way that we are. Trauma that made us pick up habits, adopt mindsets and beliefs, and erect walls within ourselves to ultimately protect us from life. Whether we realize it or not, all of those emotions from the pain follow us throughout our entire lives consciously and subconsciously.

Growing up, my parents abused drugs. This, in turn, made for a very toxic household. Along with drug use, they physically fought each other often. At four years old, I was crying, screaming at my dad to stop hitting my mom. At the age of five, I was being sexually abused in that household. I was abused again at the age of nine, which caused me to enter the foster system for the very first time. By the age of eleven, I was going into my second foster home where I was sexually abused again. As you can see, the enemy had a plan for my life.

Looking back, I now see that my childhood traumatized me. I know, only now, that God had me in the palm of His hand during those times. But major events like those at such an early age left behind scars, pain, and questions. I didn't turn to God in my pain, and even in therapy, my mind could not process all of the things that happened to me. As I continued to age, I thought I was fine, but the effects of my childhood showed up more and more as I grew into womanhood.

At the age of eighteen, I met my first love. I had severe attachment issues in this relationship that stemmed from the pain of my childhood. Growing up in a household never feeling loved, seen, and cared for made for dangerous connections. Our breakup wrecked me and triggered abandonment issues that I harbored from my parents. It sent me down a spiral. Not only was I smoking weed, I started experimenting with other drugs. Xanax, cough syrup, and even alcohol. I just wanted to escape. I would constantly black out from the drugs in my system and wake up the next day looking for my next high. I didn't want to live in the reality that was my life. My child's father came into my life around this time, and I quickly became attached to him. Our relationship fed my addictions. It fed the yearning in me that craved something, anything to make the pain stop. The deep-dwelling loneliness, old pain, and new pain—it was all so unbearable. The route that I was going, I was headed for death. But God had His own plan for my life.

It's because of pain that we run to anything that looks as if it will numb it. Something that will make it stop immediately: pacifiers. Our pacifiers usually come in the form of drugs, alcohol, and sexual impurity. We use the pleasure of sin to escape the pain of the present. To distract ourselves from it. Life can be so painful, and if trauma isn't dealt with, it manifests. You will continually choose sin instead of God over and over again until you deal with the root of your issues. So what does God say about our pain?

- Matthew 5:4 says, "Blessed are those who mourn for they will be comforted."
- Psalms 34:18 says, "The Lord is close to the brokenhearted and saves those who are crushed in spirit."

- Psalms 147:3 says, "He heals the brokenhearted and binds up their wounds."
- Psalms 27:10 says, "Though my father and mother forsake me, the Lord will receive me."

A lot of times, we rush through scripture, not really taking in what's being said. These scriptures are truth; they are promises. To truly know God's love and comfort in times of trouble is top-tier. The inexpressible joy He brings to His children when we cry out to Him is truly other dimensional. In our pain, we have to allow God to heal us. We have to allow Him in to comfort our hearts. We have to allow Him to be our peace. There is one person that you can talk to and be completely honest about everything you feel; that's Jesus. He won't judge, He won't interrupt you, He'll listen and understand. He will literally hug your heart in the midst of your prayer! When you cry out to Him, not only does the healing process begin, He begins exposing your heart and everything in it. Things from years ago that you thought you were over. He begins to break down the walls of your heart. In His presence, you can be that scared little child. You can be vulnerable. You can truly be yourself. And He will accept it all.

Only God can truly heal us from all pain and trauma. (Also, a little therapy won't hurt). Once you let Him in and allow His spirit to work, your hurt will hurt less. That gaping hole inside your heart begins to minimize. Coping mechanisms begin to dwindle. You won't need them anymore because Jesus begins to take their place. As Christians, we lean on Jesus to cope. He's our ultimate coping mechanism. The enemy uses pain to get us to turn away from God. God uses pain to get us to turn *to* Him. To be totally dependent on Him and *His* strength. Our strength fades, His is endless. So lean on Him! Sin leads to death (being apart from God). But the *gift* of God (Jesus and everything He is) leads to eternal life.

Eternal: Lasting or existing forever; without end or beginning.

This means we don't have to wait to get to heaven to experience a life of joy, peace, and comfort. Eternal life also means here and now! *Go live*!

Move Forward in Jesus's Name!

Get rid of all distractions at this time. Silence your phone, your heart, and your mind. Begin to thank God for every trauma, every painful event, every rejection, every hurt. Thank Him for each situation one by one. Welcome His presence and allow it to fill you and the room. Ask Him to show you which trauma(s) you hold on to. Which hurt drives you. Please don't rush this process; just dwell in His presence. Don't let your mind wander and don't doubt. With hands lifted, cry out to Him. Write down what He gives you and begin your healing journey.

Notes

Divine Warrior

In the beginning of my story, I never comprehended that I had authority in Jesus. I heard it so many times throughout the years, but it never clicked for me. It never occurred to me that because of Jesus, the Holy Spirit, and God's Word, I didn't have to be bullied. I didn't have to accept defeat. From the beginning of time, God's plan for us as His children was established. At the start of creation, our victory in Jesus was a sure thing. This is not an opinion of mine, it's God's truth. It's in His word. Genesis 1:26 says, "Then God said let us make mankind in our image, in our likeness, so that they may rule."

Who is God referring to when He says, "Let Us make mankind in Our image"? Well, let's break it down. What is the Holy Trinity? God, Jesus, and the Holy Spirit. Who else would God be conversing with? That means Jesus was there at the beginning of creation! Since God is eternal (without end or beginning), that says to me that Jesus had already come to earth, died, and was seated at the right hand of God before the first man was ever created! This might be hard to fathom, but God's ways are higher than our ways! We know that Jesus overcame the world through resurrection, so that means our victory over the enemy was set in stone *from the beginning*!

Being a baby in Christ, I never connected the dots. The Bible tells us to put on the full armor of God for this very reason. The enemy knows most Christians won't stand in the victory that has been freely given to them. So he continues to taunt us, to lie to us, and to make us feel powerless and inferior. The full armor of God is the armor we wear in the battle of spiritual warfare. In the battle for our souls.

The title of this chapter alone should tell you that this walk is not for wimps. We are at war, so we are called to be warriors *in* Christ.

Armor: The metal coverings formerly worn by soldiers or warriors to protect the body in battle.

We are not fighting a physical war, but a spiritual one. So the weapons we use to defend ourselves against the enemy are not weapons we can actually hold. Paul tells us in 2 Corinthians 10:3–4, "For though we live in the world, we do not wage war as the world does. The weapons we fight with are not the weapons of this world. On the contrary, they have divine power to demolish strongholds."

It wasn't until I grew older and grew closer to Jesus did I really understand this passage in Ephesians. It's hard to be chosen and be a victim. If we are called, we cannot allow the enemy to bully us. He has no rights! He just persuades us to believe he does. When Jesus died on the cross and rose again, He did so with all authority on earth and in heaven. That same authority He left with us to defeat our spiritual foes. So that means we can't fight this battle ourselves. We are only victorious through Jesus. So then, what weapons and armor are we to use as children of the Most High God?

> Finally, be strong in the Lord and in His mighty power. Put on the full armor of God, so that you can take your stand against the devil's schemes. For our struggle is not against flesh and blood, but against the rulers, against the authorities, against the powers of this dark world and against the spiritual forces of evil in the heavenly realms. Therefore put on the full armor of God, so that when the day of evil comes, you may be able to stand your ground and after you have done everything to stand, stand firm then, with the belt of truth buckled around your waist, with

the breastplate of righteousness in place, and with your feet fitted with the readiness that comes from the gospel of peace. In addition to all this, take up the shield of faith with which you can extinguish all the flaming arrows of the evil one. Take the helmet of salvation and the sword of the spirit, which is the word of God. [The Roman soldiers carried a shield, a sword, and a spear and wore groves (shin armor), his breastplate and a helmet (Padfield, D 2008).]

Belt of Truth: In biblical times, the belt in Roman soldiers' armor held everything together. What holds us together as children of God? His word, His *truth*. Obeying those laws and decrees is also truth! Walking in obedience and submission is what holds us together.

Breastplate of Righteousness: The breastplate was used to protect the heart from being pierced. We keep our hearts from being hurt by wearing Jesus as our breastplate. We are only righteous in the eyes of God *because* of Jesus's ultimate sacrifice. So we protect our hearts by continually looking to Jesus for everything and in everything.

Feet fitted with the readiness that comes from the gospel of peace: Roman soldiers wore shoes that made their footing firm, ready for battle. Our feet, our foundation should be firm in God, prepared for anything that comes our way because of the gospel of peace.

Shield of Faith: Satan will throw so many things your way to try and minimize your faith in God. The only way we block or cancel his lies is through believing. We have to know, without a doubt, that any word out of the mouth of God is the end all, be all. Not our thoughts, not our emotions, not even our circumstances. The world calls it delusion, we call it faith.

The Helmet of Salvation: What is salvation? "For God so loved the world that He gave His one and only son, that whoever believes in Him shall not perish but have eternal life" (John 3:16). We know that any helmet protects the head from injury. In the same way, the helmet of salvation protects our minds from damage. We will not lose our minds, we will not suffer from worry and anxiety, we will not perish *because* of our Savior! Quite literally, we are redeemed!

The Sword of the Spirit: The Word of God. It's how we kill Satan over and over again. It's how we hurt Him. If we don't know the Word of God, it's very easy for Him to hurt us. Every word in the Bible was inspired by God or God-breathed. That leads me to believe that every scripture can somehow be used to demolish Satan in every situation we face!

> All scripture is God-breathed and is useful for teaching,
> rebuking, correcting and training in righteousness,
> so that the servant of God may be thoroughly
> equipped for every good work.
>
> —2 Timothy 3:16–17

The Bible says every day that we should "Be alert and of sober mind because the enemy the devil prowls around like a roaring lion looking for someone to devour" (1 Peter 5:8). There is no way we can be devoured if we remember to suit ourselves in the full armor of God every day. It won't be easy. It takes practice and prayer, but remember, we were victorious at the beginning of time!

> For your sake we face death all day long; we are considered
> as sheep to be slaughtered. No, in all these things we are
> more than conquerors through him who loved us.
>
> —Romans 8:26–37

Equip Yourself

Have you ever felt like a victim to sin and/or to the enemy's tactics? In what way? Moving forward, how can you better equip yourself as a child of God?

Exercise: Every morning, before you start your day, spend thirty minutes to an hour reading your Bible. If you don't know where to start, look up scriptures and stories in the Bible on the Internet that speak to your current struggle (ex: anger, lust, faith, obedience, etc.).

Notes

A BRILLIANT CUT

A brilliant cut diamond has a specific arrangement of facets
that allows light to enter the stone and be reflected back
out in a way that creates maximum brilliance and fire.

—Adams, N. (2024)

See I have refined you though not as silver; I have
tested you in the furnace of affliction.

—Isaiah 48:10

A Brilliant Cut

This book is for the chosen. It's for the people who have never fit in. The people who got picked on or bullied. The people who couldn't understand why life just wasn't fair. Why no matter where you were at, life just felt cursed. You're not cursed, you're called. You're chosen. This book was written to help you accept it and to walk in it. Accepting chosen will be the hardest thing you'll do in life. But it will also be the most brilliant.

Only a select few understood Jesus. Only the people that were meant to accept Him, accepted Him with their whole heart. He was persecuted, talked down on, and also tempted by the enemy. Everything that we go through Jesus had to face it first. We don't serve a Master who can't empathize with what we go through. We serve one who has endless patience and understanding for our journey.

As I grow older, His love engulfs me more and more. A deeper level of understanding is gifted to me as I continue to walk with Him. Everything that I've been through has prepared me, has equipped me for who I am today. Motherless, fatherless, foster care, sexual abuse, bad choices, kids out of wedlock…It was all eventually employed to serve my purpose. To create in me righteousness, I could never acquire on my own. Going through the fire birthed in me eternal gifts of the Spirit. I am blessed. I am strong. I am confident. Not because of anything that I've done, but because of the furnace. Affliction is a gift from the Father.

God says, "See, I have refined you, though not as silver; I have tested you in the furnace of affliction."

Refine: remove impurities or unwanted elements from.

Affliction: pain or suffering

Let's replace those words with their definitions to understand this verse better.

"See I have removed impurities or unwanted elements from you, though not as silver. I have tested you in the furnace of pain and suffering." So see, not all trouble is the devil. A lot of times God allows pain and suffering to come into our lives to push us to grow. Nothing you experience is pointless. It has purpose. God is and has always been in control.

Do you know how a diamond is made? Natural diamonds are birthed under intense heat and pressure deep below the surface of the earth. Even lab-grown diamonds are produced under the same conditions. In the same way, God allows the fire to be turned up in our lives to refine us. He uses the intense pressures of life to birth us into beautiful, rare stones.

In Nicole Adam's article, "What Is a Brilliant Cut Diamond?" they describe what makes such a diamond special: "A brilliant cut diamond has a specific arrangement of facets that allows light to enter the stone and be reflected back out in a way that creates maximum brilliance and fire." God is so amazing and intentional.

In the midst of being refined for His will and purpose, we must not allow the pressure and heat force us to let go of His hand. If we let go of His hand in the furnace, there will be no diamond left to be birthed, only ashes. Ashes are fleeting and burnt up. They can't allow light in to be reflected out like a diamond. The pressure and heat from the fire removes impurities God never intended to be a part of us. Only in the furnace can we be molded into the one He's called us to be.

As you know, chosen isn't all rainbows and butterflies, it's hard. It's hard to carry your cross in a world that is in complete opposition to it. It's hard to love your enemies and those that persecute you. It's hard unlearning patterns of thinking and upheaving toxic behaviors and habits. That's an entirely different furnace in itself! But what makes this all so beautiful and so worth it is Jesus. The intimacy, the closeness, it is a privilege and an honor. To commune with the Savior of this world is beyond what we can fathom. To actually feel how much he loves and cares for you. To see how He pays attention to the tiniest of details in your life. To know He has a personality and to be able to laugh with Him is like having a secret handshake with your best friend. To know His protection, His guidance, His salvation, His interceding, and the victory we have in life itself because of Him makes it all worth it. What a beautiful burden.

We don't have to wait to come out of the fire to reflect our light back into the world. We can do it from the furnace! There are so many people waiting to hear your unique story, waiting for you to shine your light back into the world. The world needs that God-given fire and brilliance. They need to hear your testimony because they need to know Jesus. Our testimony is how we overcome, and it is also how we lead others to Him. God wants to use us, our stories, and our experiences to help the world. To help others know Him and grow closer to Him. Our call is not about our comfortability, it's about allowing God to use everything that we are. It's about becoming a vessel. That only becomes possible by first accepting the fact that you are chosen! Don't worry, God won't ignore your dreams and your desires. He knows everything you want to be in this life. "But seek first His kingdom and His righteousness and all these things will be given to you as well" (Matthew 6:33).

No more delays. It's time to walk in your calling.

Notes

A Prayer for You

Lord, I thank You for the person holding this book. I thank You that You allowed this gift to be placed in the perfect hands. I thank You for already working in their favor. I thank You for the victory that they have in Jesus to overcome the enemy and be all who You've called them to be. Lord, You know their heart and their spirit cries out for You. I speak freedom over their life. I speak overflow of the Spirit and understanding like never before God. Lord, give them the grace to be transformed. To be renewed. To be restored. Lord, I speak the blood of Jesus over their minds right now. May their entire body be Your dwelling place, God. As they seek to know more of You, God, fill them up! Lord, align their desires with Your desires and their thoughts with Your thoughts. Lord, open their eyes and their heart to receive you like never before. Lord, it's because of You this book was written and it's because of You that they will be blessed by it. We give You all the praise and honor for all of Your mighty works forever! In Jesus's name.

Amen.

About the Author

Ever since I was a little girl, I knew I'd write a book. I thought it would be strictly on my life experiences, but I'm so happy God had other plans. I grew up in Kokomo, Indiana, where big dreams like picking up and moving across the country with no family is scary and only a few do it. God allowed me to move to Atlanta, Georgia, in 2021, and it was all for His glory. With the move, He revealed to me my purpose. But I am no different than you. I am not perfect, and I'm still so honored and surprised at the fact that God decided to use me to bless others in this way. I am very much still at the beginning stages of accepting chosen myself! I am twenty-eight years young, and it took me all of my life to get here. God is not finished with me yet. This is my first book, but I see myself writing for the rest of my life. Let's grow together! Learn more about me and my life via my website or social media. Thank you so much for reading.